ZOO ANIMALS
IN THE WILD

SNAKE

JINNY JOHNSON

ILLUSTRATED BY GRAHAM ROSEWARNE

FRANKLIN WATTS
LONDON•SYDNEY

An Appleseed Editions book

First published in 2005 by Franklin Watts
96 Leonard Street, London EC2A 4XD

Franklin Watts Australia
Level 17/207 Kent Street, Sydney, NSW 2000

Created by Appleseed Editions Ltd,
Well House, Friars Hill, Guestling, East Sussex TN35 4ET

Designed by Helen James
Illustrated by Graham Rosewarne

ISBN 0 7496 5980 7

A CIP catalogue for this book is available from the British Library

Photographs by Robert E. Barber, Corbis (Anthony Bannister; Gallo Images,
Annie Griffiths Belt, Michael & Patricia Fogden, Frank Lane Picture Agency, Stephen
Frink, COLLART HERVE/CORBIS SYGMA, Linda Lewis; Frank Lane Picture Agency,
Chris Mattison; Frank Lane Picture Agency, Joe McDonald, Mary Ann McDonald,
David A. Northcott, Rob C. Nunnington; Gallo Images, Rod Patterson; Gallo Images,
Jeffery L. Rotman, Kevin Schafer, Alastair Shay; Papilio)

Printed and bound in Thailand

Contents

Snakes

Snakes are amazing creatures that manage to live in most parts of the world. Most snakes live in warm places, but some snakes live high on mountains or even in the sea.

A snake has a long body which ends in a pointed tail, but no legs or arms. Its body is not slimy. It is covered with tough, dry scales that overlap each other like the tiles on a roof. The scales help to protect the snake's body from heat and damage.

A common adder warms itself in the sun.

A python's body is covered with colourful scales.

Snakes are cold-blooded animals, which means that they can't make their own body heat. Instead, snakes lie in the sun to warm themselves and crawl into the shade to cool down.

An Australian sea snake searches for food underwater.

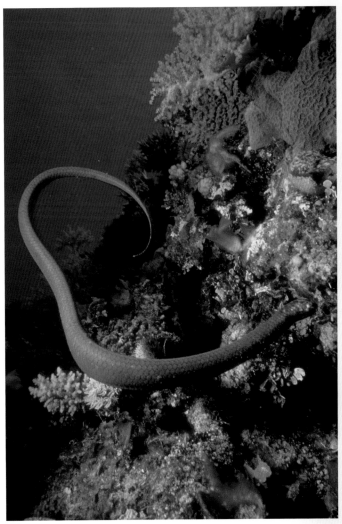

Kinds of snakes

There are about 2,700 different kinds of snakes. Some of the best known are pythons, boas, rattlesnakes and cobras. The smallest are the size of your dad's little finger. The longest is the reticulated python, which is longer than five tall adults lying head to toe.

The vine snake is one of the thinnest of all snakes.

Many different kinds of snakes are kept in zoos – including some of the biggest, such as the reticulated python and the anaconda.

A yellow anaconda.

A snake's skeleton has no leg or arm bones, but it has lots of ribs. Humans have just 12 pairs of ribs. Many snakes have more than 200 pairs.

The reticulated python is so big it can hunt animals as large as pigs.

At home in the wild

Snakes live in steamy jungles, sandy deserts and dry, rocky areas. Many climb trees, others hide in holes or cracks in rocks, and a few shelter in underground burrows. Many snakes like water.

The anaconda spends most of its life in rivers and moves faster in water than on land.

Some snakes move around to find food during the day.

Horned vipers live in the desert sands of Africa.

Others come out only at night. Snakes spend much of their time resting between meals.

A snake's skin gets worn and damaged as it moves. Several times a year, a snake sheds its outer skin. It rubs its head on the ground to loosen the skin, then crawls out of it, leaving it inside out on the ground.

A Malagasy cat-eye tree snake.

Like other snakes, a rat snake sheds its skin all at once.

At home in the zoo

A snake's home in a zoo doesn't need to be very big, but it should be about the same temperature as its home in the wild. The enclosure should be at least two-thirds the length of the snake's body and should have rocks or branches for the snake to slither on.

Most snake enclosures have glass fronts so visitors can look at the snakes safely.

A monocled cobra in Denver zoo.

A zoo snake also needs something rough to rub against when it's time to shed its skin.

All zoo snakes need some water in their home. Many snakes like to have a pool large enough to swim or soak in.

An anaconda enjoys a dip in the pool in its enclosure.

Finding food

All snakes catch and eat other creatures. Some snakes go out and hunt for their food. Others simply lie in wait for their prey. They stay hidden until an animal such as a lizard, frog or worm comes near, then dart forward to seize it in their jaws.

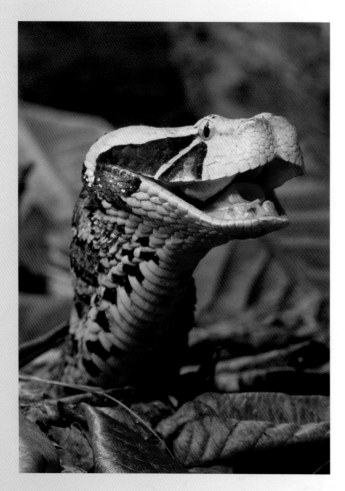

Snakes cannot chew, so they must swallow their food whole.

Boas and pythons eat animals such as mice, rats, and rabbits. They kill their prey by constriction – the snake wraps its body around

A Gaboon viper ready to strike.

Most zoo snakes are fed once a week. They're usually given dead rats and mice to eat. Sometimes zookeepers jiggle the food around to make the snakes want to catch it.

The big bulge in this African egg-eating snake's body is an egg it has just swallowed.

the animal and squeezes until it stops breathing. Then the snake can take its time swallowing its catch.

Most snakes don't need to eat every day. The biggest pythons and boas may eat only a few large animals – such as pigs or deer – a year.

Poisonous snakes

Only about 400 kinds of snakes are poisonous. About half of these – including cobras, vipers, adders and rattlesnakes – are dangerous to people. A poisonous snake uses its venom, or poison, to kill prey before swallowing it.

The snake's poison is made in glands in its head or body. The glands are linked to large, hollow teeth called fangs. When the snake bites, poison flows from its glands into the fangs and is injected into the prey.

A green mamba about to seize its prey in its poisonous fangs.

A poisonous snake may also bite anything that attacks or disturbs it. Some cobras spit poison to warn off enemies.

A cobra spits its venom at an enemy.

The Gaboon viper has the largest fangs of any poisonous snake.

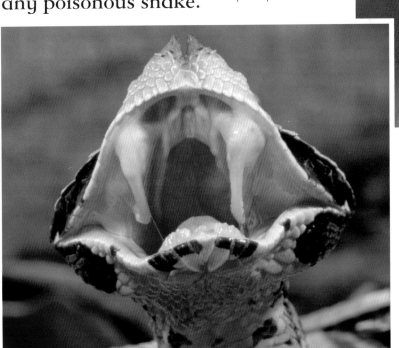

When they're feeding poisonous snakes, zookeepers hold the food on long tongs to avoid being bitten.

Moving

It might seem hard to move around without legs, but snakes are very good at it. The black mamba snake can move faster than a human can run.

Snakes have different ways of moving on the ground. Some move in a straight line by pushing against the ground with big scales on their body. Others move in S-shaped curves. They push at the points where their body bends.

A sidewinder adder slithers across sand dunes in the desert.

Snakes are easy to keep in zoos because they don't mind not being able to travel very far. They just need some rocks and branches to slither over.

A green tree python wraps its strong coils around a branch.

Most snakes can climb trees. Some, such as the green tree python, are extra good at climbing because they have a grasping tail. The snake can use its tail to hold on to branches.

A paradise tree snake can jump from a branch and glide to another tree.

17

Staying safe

Most snakes, except for the very biggest, have enemies. Birds, mammals and even other snakes will eat them. Many snakes try to stay safe by staying out of sight. The colours of some snakes help them to blend in with fallen leaves on the ground or twigs on trees.

A Gaboon viper lies among fallen leaves. Its colour and pattern look like the leaves, making the snake hard to see.

A secretary bird catches a snake with its feet.

Every time a rattlesnake moults, another ring is added to its rattle.

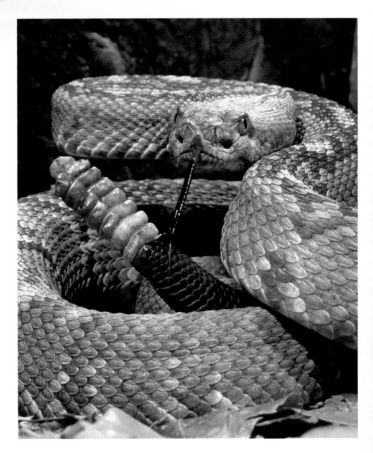

The cobra scares off enemies by making itself look bigger. It has loose skin on either side of its head. When it's disturbed, the cobra spreads out this skin, making its head look more threatening.

The rattlesnake shakes the rattle at the end of its tail as a warning. The rattle is made of rings of hardened scales and makes a buzzing noise when shaken.

Eggs and young

Most snakes lay eggs. They lay them
in hollows in the ground and cover them
with earth and leaves to keep them warm.
Then most snakes leave their eggs.

A few snakes, such as the Indian python,
look after their eggs more carefully.
The mother snake curls round her
eggs and keeps them warm
with her body until they
are ready to hatch.

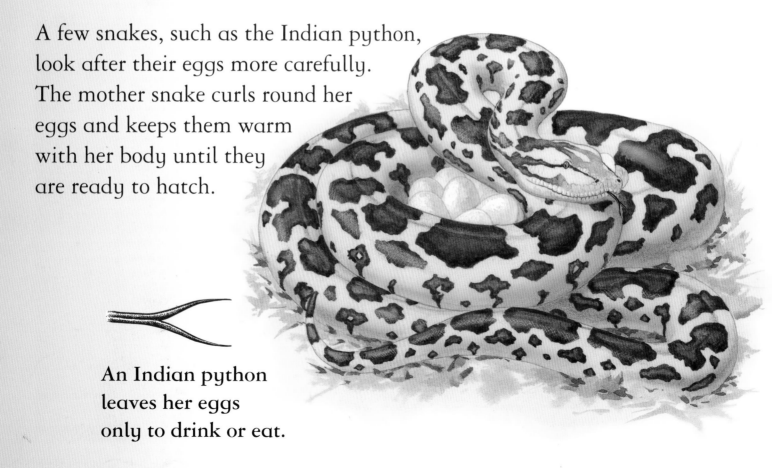

An Indian python
leaves her eggs
only to drink or eat.

When the young snakes hatch, they look like tiny adult snakes. Snakes don't live in families, so the young start taking care of themselves and finding their own food straight away.

A baby snake has an egg tooth to help it break out of its egg.

A mother snake has left these eggs to hatch out on their own.

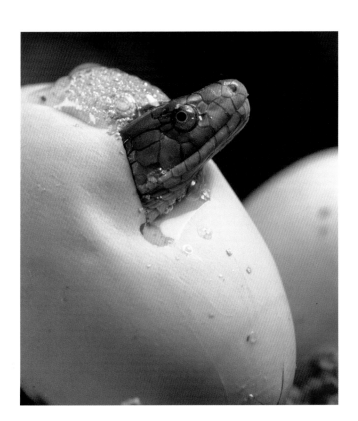

Zoo snakes are given nesting boxes where they can lay their eggs and cover them with straw. Sometimes eggs may be taken away and kept warm in an incubator, especially if the snake is a very rare kind.

Live young

Some snakes don't lay eggs. Instead, the mother keeps the eggs inside her body while they develop. The eggs don't have a shell but are covered by an outer skin called a membrane. When the young are ready to hatch, the eggs are pushed out of the mother's body. The young then break their way out of the outer skin.

When young snakes are born live in the zoo, they are taken from their mother and put in their own enclosures straight away.

The anaconda (left) gives birth to its young in this way. The mother keeps about 20 to 40 young inside her as they grow. When the snakes hatch, they are about 60 cm long.

A boa constrictor keeps her eggs inside her body until they are ready to hatch.

23

Snake senses

Like other animals, snakes need to see, hear and smell to move around and find food. Snakes don't have eyelids, so they can't blink. They can see movement well, but they probably can't see much else.

Snakes don't have ears on the outside of their bodies. But they can hear some sounds, and they can pick up the feeling of movements on the ground.

Sight is much more important than hearing for most snakes, including this black mamba.

A snake's sense of smell is very good. As well as smelling with its nose, a snake flicks its forked tongue in and out to pick up smells from the air, water, or ground. This helps a snake track its prey and stay away from enemies.

The parrot snake hunts frogs in South American jungles.

A rhinoceros viper explores the world with its forked tongue.

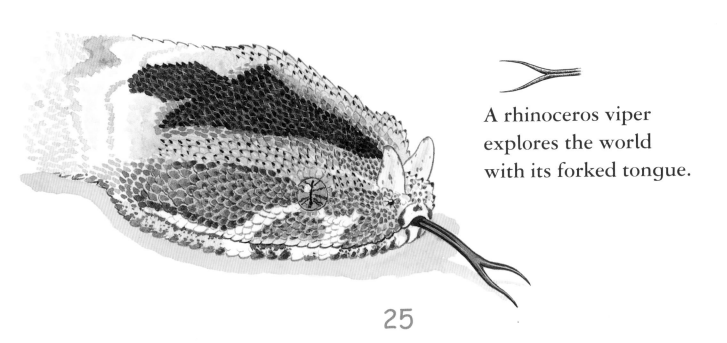

Special senses

Many snakes can sense the heat given off by other animals. Some, such as rattlesnakes and pit vipers, have a special way of finding prey. These snakes have a deep pit on either side of their heads between the nose and eyes.

This rattlesnake is about to catch a mouse it has tracked down by sensing its heat.

Pit vipers are named for the heat-sensing pit near their eyes.

The pits allow the snake to sense the heat given off by animals such as rats and mice and to work out where the animals are. So the snake can track down its food even on the darkest night.

Snake fact file

Here is some more information about snakes.
Your mum or dad might like to read this,
or you could read these pages together.

Snakes belong to a group of animals called reptiles. Some
of the main types of snakes are boas, pythons, king snakes,
garter snakes, rattlesnakes, mambas, cobras and vipers.

Size

One of the smallest snakes is the Brahminy blind snake, which
is only 5 cm long and weighs just a few grams. Many thread
snakes are only 7.5 cm long. The biggest snakes are the
anaconda and the reticulated python. The anaconda lives
in South American jungles and can be up to 10 metres long,
although not all anacondas reach this size. It can weigh up
to 150 kg. The reticulated python, which lives in Asia, is also
about 10 metres long but is not as heavy as the anaconda.

Where snakes live

Snakes live in most parts of the world, but more live in tropical
countries than anywhere else. There are no snakes in Iceland,
Antarctica, New Zealand, Greenland or Ireland.

Snake numbers

There are plenty of most kinds of snakes, but there are at least 70 different types that are rare or becoming rare. There are two main reasons for this. First, some of the places where snakes live, such as tropical forests, are being destroyed. Second, many snakes are caught and sold as pets or killed for their skin.

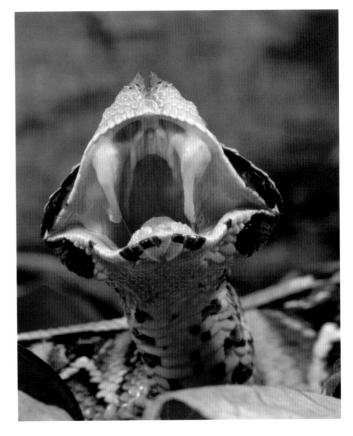

Find out more

If you want to know more about snakes check out these websites.

Smithsonian National Zoological Park: Snakes
http://nationalzoo.si.edu/Animals/ReptilesAmphibians/Herps.cfm?type=snake

San Diego Zoo: Reptiles
http://www.sandiegozoo.org/animalbytes/a-reptiles.html

Indianapolis Zoo: Snakes
http://www.indyzoo.com/content.aspx?cid=436

Words to remember

enclosure
The area where an animal lives in a zoo.

gland
A part of the body that makes a special substance, such as poison in snakes.

incubator
A machine for keeping eggs warm until they hatch.

prey
An animal that is hunted and eaten by another animal.

reptile
A cold-blooded animal that has a backbone.

scales
Hard pieces of skin that cover a reptile's body.

skeleton
The bony framework of the body.

tropical
The parts of the world around the equator where it is always hot.

Index